The Productivity Mindset

The Productivity Mindset

How to Improve Focus, Combat Laziness, and Increase Productivity

Mindset Reading

JAICO PUBLISHING HOUSE

Ahmedabad Bangalore Chennai
Delhi Hyderabad Kolkata Mumbai

Published by Jaico Publishing House
A-2 Jash Chambers, 7-A Sir Phirozshah Mehta Road
Fort, Mumbai - 400 001
jaicopub@jaicobooks.com
www.jaicobooks.com

THE PRODUCTIVITY MINDSET
ISBN 978-81-988454-4-3

First Jaico Impression: 2025

Page design and layout by R. Ajith Kumar, Delhi

Printed by
Parksons Graphics Pvt. Ltd., Mumbai

To,

Satguru Mata Sudiksha Ji Maharaj.

Your divine guidance and blessings have been the light on my path and the strength behind my journey. Through your teachings, I have learned the value of self-discipline, focus, and living with purpose.

This book is a humble offering, made possible only by your constant presence in my life and in the hearts of my family.

CONTENTS

Introduction ix

1. Off to a Productive Start! 1
2. The Laziness Trap 13
3. Stop Delaying, Start Doing 23
4. Peak Performance State 37
5. Master Mental Toughness 46
6. 10 Ways to Master Daily Productivity 55
7. Quality vs. Quantity 69
8. Focus Through Meditation 77
9. Power of the Right Mindset 87
10. The Art of Doing Nothing 91
11. 17 Habits of Highly Productive People 100
12. 27 Life Lessons from 27 Years of My Life 109

About the Author 127

INTRODUCTION

I have struggled with being productive for a long time. There were days when I felt motivated, but couldn't focus or do anything. I'd plan my day, but still end up wasting time on things that didn't matter. I used to beat myself up for my laziness and procrastination, wondering if something was wrong with me. However, over time, I began to notice a pattern. It wasn't a lack of willpower; it was a lack of a productive routine, good habits, and self-awareness. Once I started understanding how my brain worked and how habits are formed, everything began to change.

Through a lot of trial and error, I discovered what actually worked for me. I started waking up with clarity, working with intention, and ending my days with a sense of fulfilment. That personal transformation is what motivated me to write this book. I wanted to share the tools, frameworks, and insights that helped me so that you can experience the same kind of shift.

After writing my first book, *Master Your Mindset*, I received an overwhelming response from readers who wanted to know how to make the best use of the right mindset into daily life, especially when it comes to overcoming distractions and being productive. That book focused on building inner strength, clarity, and emotional control. But I realized something important: having the right mindset is only one part of the puzzle; the other part is action.

This second book was born out of that realization. If *Master Your Mindset* is about shaping your thoughts, then this book is about shaping your actions. It's a natural follow-up, focusing not just on how we think but on how we use our time, energy, and attention to turn those thoughts into results. While mindset builds the foundation, productivity builds the structure of a successful life. And I wanted to help readers move from understanding to execution.

Productivity isn't merely about accomplishing your tasks on time; it's also about doing meaningful work with right intentions. Most people believe being productive means getting more work done in less time. However, it's about working smarter and knowing when to prioritise your most important tasks.

In today's digital age, people are increasingly overwhelmed with distractions, laziness, and procrastination. This book is designed to help you break free from these struggles and develop a right mindset to achieve peak productivity.

When you're overwhelmed with work or deadlines, you most definitely don't tend to enjoy it. This book will tell you how you can make such daunting tasks enjoyable. It mainly focuses on overcoming laziness, making tough choices, and balancing your mind to stay focused and productive. My favourite chapters in this book are *The Laziness Trap, Focus Through Meditation, Peak Performance State*, and *27 Life Lessons.*

I've battled with laziness more times than I can count. It wasn't until I understood the science and psychology behind it that I could break free from its grip. Writing *The Laziness Trap* helped me reflect on those moments and enabled me to share real strategies that actually worked for me.

Productivity isn't always about doing more. Sometimes, it's about slowing down, being still, and reconnecting with your thoughts. Meditation has helped me clear my mind, reduce stress, and focus better. In *Focus Through Meditation,* I have talked about various ways to improve your focus through meditation. This chapter is an invitation for readers to experience the same clarity.

Peak performance state, also known as the flow state, is something I've always admired in high performers. The idea of being so focused that everything else fades away fascinated me. I wanted to understand how to reach that state consistently, and this chapter—*Peak Performance State*—explores what I've learned and how anyone can access it.

27 Life Lessons was one of the most enjoyable and reflective chapters to write. It's a collection of powerful insights I've gathered over the years—lessons that have shaped who I am and how I approach life and productivity. I hope readers find at least one lesson that resonates deeply with them.

One of the main behavioural traits that hinders productivity is procrastination. Waiting for the "perfect moment" causes many people to put off crucial tasks. But that ideal time never arrives. Lack of right approach and attitude is the problem here, not a lack of time.

Fear, perfectionism, and a lack of drive are the main causes of procrastination. This book will show you how to stop putting off crucial tasks and begin acting on them right now.

One of the most significant themes in this book is the growth mindset, which argues that you can develop this mindset with effort and practice. Many people feel that being productive is a unique quality; however, they are wrong. Anyone who is willing to make small, consistent improvements can build the habit of being productive.

Reading about productivity is not enough. The key to transformation is taking action. This book contains straightforward, doable measures that you can take right now to increase your productivity. The techniques in this book will help you take charge of your time and energy, whether establishing a reliable daily regimen, learning self-discipline, or getting rid of distractions.

The end goal should not be to become perfect; it should be to achieve steady progress. If you apply the principles mentioned in this book, you will gradually be able to develop the habits and mindset of a highly productive person.

So, are you ready to break free from procrastination, increase your focus, and achieve your most important goals? If yes, then let's get started.

1

OFF TO A PRODUCTIVE START!

Growing up, I was never a morning person. For several years, I hated waking up early. My circadian rhythm was tuned in such a way that I used to get headaches if I had to wake up early and to do anything at all. This routine went on for years, until I realised that I had to change it. Naturally, this began impacting my life negatively as my productivity decreased.

Somewhere in the back of my mind, I knew I had to change this routine to make any positive change in my life. Initial days were extremely tough. I used to wake up early only to return to the sweet comfort of sleep in half an hour.

I was aware that this habit of waking up late would not change suddenly. I had to take it slow and look for habits, mechanisms, and ideas that would help me wake up early and have a productive start for the day. I will share some of them with you:

Make your bed as soon as you wake up

Just form this one habit of making your bed soon after you wake up in the morning, and notice how your entire day goes by.

Early mornings are known to have a positive impact on our brain and mood. You will notice that you are mostly—especially on the days when you have slept well—in a calm state of mind in the mornings as compared to the evenings. So, if you take your very first decision (of making your bed) in the morning soon after you wake up with a disciplined mind, it sets the tone for the rest of your day.

This was one of the many crucial lessons I learned from the book *Make Your Bed* by retired United States Navy admiral William H. McRaven. I really enjoyed this book, and if I had to sum up its message in one line, it would be:

> *"If you want to change the world, start off by making your bed." - William H. McRaven*

This is one of the most thought-provoking lines from the book. It inspires tremendous motivation and discipline. Who doesn't want to turn their lives around? Who doesn't wish to make a difference in society? Everyone in this world today is struggling with something or the other, fighting their own battles, and also wishing to change themselves for good.

Why not start your journey towards attaining a productive mindset with this simple habit of making your bed?

Plan your day the night before

Always plan your next day the night before. This will help you recall all your pending tasks for the coming day. You can even write these tasks down so that when you revisit them in the morning, you would be better prepared for the day.

You can also take this one step further and visualize yourself completing these tasks. Imagine yourself as a third person performing those tasks and finishing them one at a time.

It's a powerful visualization technique, and will take just takes five minutes of your time. Follow this technique every night and go to sleep. You will notice a positive energy flowing in to complete those tasks the next morning.

Prioritise your most important tasks

Our mind works the way we want it to. So, if you list all your tasks for the next day the night before, your mind will already remember that you must do this much work and it will prepare for it by itself.

You just need to decide on which task you want to do as early as possible. If you finish your most important task early on, you will save more time for another task that is not quite important to you.

Prioritising your tasks is necessary when you have a huge list of tasks to accomplish. Doing your most important tasks early also releases stress from your brain to do more stuff.

YOUR PRODUCTIVE TIME SHOULD BE LIKE THE TIME YOU LOVE SPENDING WITH YOUR BEST FRIEND.

Importance of exercise and nutrition

It all comes down to the unique hold your mind has over your body. The better your mental well-being, the more focused you are on your tasks. Productivity is meaningless if you are not physically and mentally well. It not only saps your energy physically and leaves you tired but also distracts you from anything you try to do.

Keep your body and mind healthy enough to carry out your daily tasks with a positive mindset. If you have a well-balanced body, mind, and soul, you can do anything in this world. However, to achieve this, you require a disciplined lifestyle.

Internalise the change you would like to see in yourself. Don't wait for motivation to inspire you. Motivation is fleeting. For instance, if you watch a motivational video, its effect will last on your mind for only a few minutes or some days. Besides, it won't have any tangible positive impact on your mind and body. You will need to keep seeking such methods to boost your motivation whenever you feel demoralised. That is why you should try to seek intrinsic motivation, rather than extrinsic.

If you truly believe in yourself, you won't need any kind of extrinsic motivation to give you that push. However, you need to develop a mindset for intrinsic motivation that will help you stay inspired.

INTERNALISE THE CHANGE YOU WOULD LIKE TO SEE IN YOURSELF.

Mental clarity and journaling

Have you ever maintained a journal? If not, then I strongly recommend you to start doing it at once. I have experienced that writing down all your thoughts and feelings—anything that's going on in your mind or you're going through—on a piece of paper helps you calm down and gain mental clarity and focus.

Sitting at one place and writing down your thoughts and emotions in a journal is similar to taking a therapy session. Like how you share your distress with your therapist, you pour all your thoughts in a journal. If you stay consistent with this habit, it will certainly benefit you for years to come. It unburdens you, reduces your stress and anxiety, and enables you to process your feelings and thoughts better.

In the process, you will see that this habit will boost your mood and productivity. It not only enhances your creativity and helps you calm down as you write your feelings and emotions, it also enables you build a strong relationship with yourself.

We all deal with anxiety and depression in some way or another. I admit that it varies from person to person. However, if you willingly take care of yourself and learn about the connection between your mind and emotions, these struggles will gradually decrease.

Carry a little journal with you wherever you go. Write down any curious thought you think is worth noting. Just pen them down as they come to your mind. The purpose of maintaining a journal is to process your raw thoughts, emotions, and feelings on the page so that you can reflect on them when you read the journal again later.

If you develop this simple habit of journaling and stay consistent with it, you will notice a significant change in your mindset. It will not only boost your intrinsic motivation but also enhance your productivity in whichever task you undertake. You will also notice a significant improvement in your mental clarity and decision-making ability.

So, start journaling!

Live like you own the day

No one can help you to stand out or do something unique. You have to do it for yourself. You can always do that through reading, learning from a mentor, and referring to online resources. However, it is always *you* who needs to make the first move. Otherwise, nothing will change.

Remember, it will always be *you* who has to fight the battle alone. To bring about change in yourself and the world, you must first make some sacrifices.

For instance, let go of the bad habits you have built over the years—*now* is the time to change and take charge of the day! This is your moment! Start by simply making your bed in the morning, or it could be anything. Just make sure you follow this one habit for several days and months in a row.

Gradually, you will realise that you have begun to own your day, and you feel focused and productive all day long. Such habits should be fun, not boring as if you're struggling to complete a chore.

Another way to look at it is: Treat your productive time as if you're spending it with your best friend. This way, you won't feel like staying unproductive throughout the day because you would already be in a calm and happy mood. Just as you are with your best buddy.

2

THE LAZINESS TRAP

Do you often find yourself whiling away your time and hoping for a quick and easy way out of all your tasks? Do you often neglect your responsibilities and make excuses to avoid taking any action? This is because most of us enjoy lazing around and doing nothing rather than actually getting up and working. And if you enjoy doing nothing, you get used to it. You slowly fall into that laziness trap—without even realizing it.

A part of us always feels lazy in some way or another to do certain tasks, while another part truly wishes to overcome that laziness and get things done. To beat this feeling, we need to first understand where it comes from—only then can we work on ways to break free from it and stay productive.

Lack of motivation or purpose

When you lack motivation or purpose, your brain signals you to avoid the task, and you use that as an excuse to not act at all. Over time, this action becomes a habit, and eventually, it leads to perpetual laziness. You also don't feel guilty about not accomplishing that task.

Your lack of purpose and unwillingness to put in any effort to do meaningful work will naturally stop you from achieving your set goals. That's why it's crucial to learn how to get going and complete your tasks—no matter how lazy or demotivated you feel in that moment.

Many people face this issue, but they try to overcome this habit by doing the work they enjoy the most; they seek their true purpose in life. This is a simple but effective method to break through laziness. But this helps only for the time being. It not only temporarily distracts your brain from its lazy patterns but also motivates you to focus on your crucial tasks.

This method, however, works gradually. If you stay consistent, your mind will learn to adapt and you will begin to improve faster. Remember, your brain can learn anything quickly if you practise it daily.

Sometimes, you avoid doing any task because of boredom or low energy, and this avoidance makes you lazy as the time passes. However, you can fight these feelings if you set your mind to achieve bigger goals in life.

Focus on achieving what truly matters to you, because you can deal with laziness but you cannot bring back lost time. So, act on your goals before time passes you by.

YOUR BRAIN CAN LEARN ANYTHING QUICKLY IF YOU PRACTISE IT DAILY.

Build good habits to combat laziness

Building good habits is one of the best ways to overcome laziness. Start with small actions, such as breaking down big tasks into small, manageable ones. This way you can accomplish them, one task at a time. Planning your day the night before, limiting your screen time, and avoiding any kind of distraction also helps.

These habits take months to build, but once you have formed the habit and stayed consistent, your body and mind will effectively be able to combat laziness. You will never know how to fight laziness if you don't act, and you take action by building habits.

I did the same to deal with my laziness. Whenever I feel too lazy to work, I do what I like doing the most—I write a paragraph about what's going on in my daily life—my favourite activity, and suddenly my brain becomes active. I have noticed this a lot; if you do your favourite activity whenever you feel lazy, your mind loves it and suddenly becomes active.

Now, your active mind tricks you into thinking that you will be able to complete the other pending tasks, too, which are important and urgent.

Remember, you just need a little push to start your work. While this may seem boring at first, once you build a momentum, you are good to go.

Also, always surrounding yourself with active people who inspire you will help change your passive energy into an active one. This change of environment will eventually make you more active and productive. You need to take such steps to trick your brain and lead a productive life.

So, stop being lazy and get to work!

BUILDING GOOD HABITS IS ONE OF THE BEST WAYS TO OVERCOME LAZINESS.

My struggle with laziness

I have failed many times when it came to completing tasks that were important to me. Even though I knew they were necessary, I would intentionally avoid doing them. I would lack motivation to get up from my bed in the mornings and think about the pending tasks. I was so lazy that I never thought about the consequences—how avoiding them will affect me both internally and externally.

Over time, however, I managed to break free from that laziness trap in my daily routine. What helped me was finding some intrinsic motivation to get things done. One method I used was a small reward system. Every time I completed a task, I would head out for a nice 15-minute walk, browse social media, or enjoy a cup of coffee, and so on. I treated them as small rewards. This method proved to be quite effective when I was struggling with laziness.

Another technique that helped me was learning how to distract my mind from resistance and shifting my focus completely on the work I needed to do. You have to train your brain to do hard things. It takes a lot of time and patience to build that discipline, but it's worth the effort.

I have realised that the brain naturally chooses easy tasks—the ones that do not take much time and effort on your part. That's why you do them happily. However, these tasks rarely give you any satisfaction. If you wish to grow, you need to take on harder challenges and let your mind know that you are capable of doing difficult things as well.

If you want to combat laziness, you must learn to challenge your brain. This requires training both your brain and body—through practices like meditation.

I practised meditation for a year, and it helped me tremendously, especially with maintaining focus and calm. So many people practise meditation to transform their mental and physical well-being. It is one of the most effective tools I have come to realise, and I genuinely enjoy doing it every day.

When you are calm and stress-free, you can get anything done. Most of the time, you struggle with self-doubt and feel demotivated, that's why you can't do the things you want to do. Meditation can help you boost your motivation, regulate your emotions, and make you feel good about your mind and body. And when you feel good internally, you're more likely to do the tasks you usually avoid doing. There are several ways to overcome laziness, but meditation I believe is the easiest and effective one.

If you notice, when you feel good about yourself, you become productive and everything around you eventually improves as well.

So, how can you make yourself feel good and happy most of the time? That is something you will have to reflect on your own, because every individual is different. Look within and figure out what makes you happy. You may enjoy different activities to feel good about yourself—unlike me, who likes to journal about my daily life. Everyone simply has to figure out what makes them feel good about themselves by looking within.

3

STOP DELAYING, START DOING

To be honest with you, I am someone who procrastinates a lot. Most of the time, I don't feel like doing any work, even when the task in question is important. However, in the end, I am aware that I must do that work even if I don't feel like doing it.

Think about it: Why don't you like doing a particular task? Is it because of your lack of interest? Or is it because you feel demotivated, confused, or stressed? For this, you must truly understand what procrastination means.

Often, procrastination is confused with laziness and is the result of our fear of facing unexpected problems or failure—even before we take any action. This fear stops us from putting in any effort to complete our tasks and also leaves us feeling demotivated and stressed.

If you think too much about failure or anticipate problems before you even begin, you will only hold yourself back from doing anything productive. Avoiding your tasks won't make you immune to failure, because, this way, you will never do anything at all.

Our brain is wired to seek instant gratification; it makes us temporarily feel good because of the dopamine (feel-good hormone) release. This dopamine release keeps us addicted to the temporary pleasures. But if we trick our brain to focus on long-term goals, we'll be able to overcome procrastination, and eventually our brain will stop seeking instant pleasure.

However, the problem here is: our dopamine-seeking brain will always trick us into avoiding any productive work by distracting us with things that give us temporary pleasure (for e.g., putting off studying till the last minute, doomscrolling on Instagram, or impulsive online shopping). This consequently makes us anxious and highly self-aware of not being able to do the task, eventually leading to procrastination. You must become aware of this and do the complete opposite.

This game of procrastination starts with your mind. If you learn how to work around these temptations, you can easily discipline your mind.

So, tell me something: are you a chronic procrastinator? Do you repeatedly delay or postpone your tasks despite knowing how important they are? Do you struggle to complete a task because you want it to be perfect no matter how long it might take? The answers to these questions are in identifying what's missing in your approach towards any work.

Interestingly, I have noticed that for many people, the missing element is fun. All of us want to enjoy the work we do. Nobody likes it when their work turns into a burden. We are less likely to procrastinate if we truly enjoy doing a particular task, rather than feel demotivated and keep it for later.

So, how to stop procrastinating and actually have fun while working?

Slice it down

We don't eat an entire pizza in a single bite—we eat it slice by slice, right? Eating a large one at once would be quite uncomfortable unless it's a mini, bite-sized pizza. Similarly, a big, daunting task becomes easier when we break it into smaller ones. Just like you never eat a large pizza in one go, don't try to finish an entire task all at once—take it one slice at a time.

Even if you intend on completing your entire task in one attempt, you will make lots of mistakes, because you'll be distracted with the pressure that comes along with completion of the task. So, it will be a wise choice to carry out your tasks one by one.

Productivity isn't just about finishing your to-do list; it also means being actively engaged in your tasks and enjoying the process so you don't feel tired or drained by the end of the day.

We live in a fast-paced world, and everyone is in a rush to complete one task after another in order to show how productive they are. No one wants to slow down and relax. However, slowing down your process makes you even more productive because of the time you put in. This not only improves your focus but also reduces your burnout. That said, you can afford to slow down only if you don't procrastinate. And to avoid procrastination, you should start by slicing down your bigger tasks into smaller ones like I previously mentioned.

Not only will this help you complete the task at hand but you will also be able to strategize your next task better.

Time blocking

One of the reasons why you procrastinate is because you don't have a proper plan and time management system. There are a lot of strategies you can use to combat procrastination, but if you can't manage your time effectively, you will never be able to increase your productivity.

Time blocking is one of the best methods of time management to effectively combat procrastination. It is when you schedule your daily tasks into dedicated blocks of time. It is a strategy where you effectively manage to complete your task according to the time you have scheduled for it. Set the time aside for your task based on its priority.

For instance:
10 a.m. to 11 a.m.: Check and respond to mails
11 a.m. to 1 p.m.: Working on Project A
1 p.m. to 2 p.m.: Lunch hour
2 p.m. to 3 p.m.: Attend a meeting
3 p.m. to 4 p.m.: Finalise work on Project B
4 p.m. to 4.30 p.m.: Evening break
4.30 p.m. to 5.45 p.m.: Finish other small tasks
5.45 p.m. to 6 p.m.: Wrap-up or plan for the next day

To try this method, you can use resources that are easily available around you, such as your daily calendar, time management apps, productivity apps, a simple note-taking system, etc.

If you're a multitasker, you are quite likely to feel exhausted, burnt out, and distracted from your tasks if you are unable to manage your time efficiently. Time blocking technique is extremely useful for those who juggle multiple jobs on a daily basis. This not only reduces your stress when it comes to decision-making but also helps you maintain a structured life. If you lack focus and discipline, then you should definitely try this time blocking method.

Try it out every day for the next 30 days, and see how effectively it works for you.

Limit distractions

When you are working on something, it's important to fully focus on that task. However, you will often find yourself distracted by several things that steal your attention.

Your focus naturally increases when there are no distractions. So, make sure that when you sit down to work, no one can distract you.

It's in your hands to limit those distractions. You can put your phone on silent mode, leave a noisy room and move to a quiet place where you find peace. This approach will help you to complete your task with complete focus.

Delegate tasks

If you think delegation decreases your productivity, you may be wrong. In fact, delegating your tasks increases your productivity—it frees up your time so that you can do more of the things you like.

Delegating your tasks is an essential technique that everyone should consider. Many productivity experts rely on the method of delegation to ease their workflow. This also allows them to work on other high-priority commitments that need their immediate attention, and ideas that they would like to explore.

SLICE YOUR BIG TASK INTO SMALL CHUNKS.

For instance, if you're managing a team, try delegating your mundane tasks to someone you trust and will be able to do this task without your supervision. This frees up your time to focus on more creative work you might want to pursue. Working on a creative task not only sharpens your mind but also inspires you to think of fresh ideas, enhancing your overall output.

Most entrepreneurs and successful people use this as an effective way to free up their minds and stay focused on what truly matters to them.

Reward yourself

When was the last time you rewarded yourself for completing a task? Rewarding yourself is one of the most effective ways to feel good about working on any tasks. Think about it: if you feel rewarded, won't you naturally look forward to working on other tasks?

It can be refreshing and fun to reward yourself after you finish a task. Whether the task is simple or challenging, make sure you treat yourself to something you like once it's completed.

Your reward can be anything that lifts your spirits—taking a quick break, going for a walk, or talking to your friends. A five-minute reward after 30 minutes of focussed work on a task works wonders.

This productivity technique is both practical and useful. A lot of people have used it to complete their work on time without feeling frustrated or lazy in the process.

YOU FOCUS BETTER WHEN THERE ARE NO DISTRACTIONS.

Overcoming fatigue

We all feel tired at some point of the day. Our body feels exhausted for one reason or another. You may be doing a lot of work, especially physical work which can somehow affect your body and exhaust you.

Apart from physical exertion, we also feel tired if we are mentally stressed. Some tasks demand a lot of your mental energy. And all you need at this point is to rest and a good sleep for your mind and body to recuperate.

I'm no stranger to this fatigue and tiredness. Make sure you correct your sleeping cycle and get enough sleep to repair your body. Lack of rest feels like a bad hangover. It hurts your eyes and brain, makes you groggy and lethargic.

Most of the time, a good amount of rest and sleep helps you overcome your tiredness. You then feel motivated enough to act when it's needed the most.

Work with sincere intentions when you've given your body the rest it deserves. It is only then you will be able to do your tasks productively.

Know your purpose

Most of the time, people don't know what they want in life; they are so lost that they just keep living without any set goals or plans. This will only intensify their anxiety and fear of failure, eventually turning them into chronic procrastinators.

Knowing your purpose will help you gain clarity. Define your goals specifically, find meaning in your work, and design a roadmap of how you aim to get there.

So, whenever you feel distracted and lost, ask yourself: what do you truly want in life, what is your *purpose*? What is it that makes you happy?

There's a quote on this by Brian Tracy that truly stuck with me:

> *"Lack of clarity is the number-one time-waster. Always be asking, 'What am I trying to do? How am I trying to do it?'"*

4

PEAK PERFORMANCE STATE

We all have a lot to do in our lives. But sometimes, whether it's a job, a task, or a routine responsibility, it can feel like you are trapped in the system—with no way out.

The psychology behind it isn't very complicated to understand. It's actually quite simple: you must be deeply involved in whatever you do.

Take up tasks that do not feel like work. You must learn to love the process.

Have you ever wondered why some people don't get tired of their work? It's because they truly love their job. It's the highlight of their day. Some even go to bed at night looking forward to doing their favourite thing the next morning.

It's not difficult to reach this stage—you simply have to identify what your favourite thing is. The "flow state" is nothing more than doing your favourite thing and deeply enjoying the process.

It may take some time to figure out what is it that you enjoy the most. But once you do, it just feels incredible. I'm not kidding—when you are in a flow state, you can finish five hours of work in just one. This is when your performance truly peaks. So, let's first understand what a flow state is.

What is a flow state?

The flow state is a state of mind where you are so involved in a particular activity that nothing can distract you. Have you ever had this experience where you suddenly find yourself in a flow state and lose track of time while doing a particular work?

This happens when you do your favourite activity. For example, you love writing, and when you sit down to write, you find yourself deeply immersed in the process of writing. You lose sense of time because you are now into a flow state, and ideas keep flowing into your mind, naturally and effortlessly.

A flow state is something that's common among creative people, such as artists, performers, eccentric thinkers, who love to express themselves and generate new ideas.

When you enter a flow state, your mind becomes highly productive. It's like a good workout for your brain because when you think creatively, your mind generates patterns faster than usual. Your mind enters into a productive zone when you are in a flow state.

I believe there are many ways to stay productive and get things done faster. But productivity isn't simply about how fast you are in completing the task. The crucial aspect of being productive is enjoying the task you undertake, with a calm and stress-free mind.

The flow state is one of the most productive and effortless ways to complete your work. Writing, for example, is one of my favourite tasks of the day. When I write, I naturally slip into the flow state, without any effort.

Why is the flow state necessary for your work?

Believe it or not, but every task you work on requires you to be in a flow state. And once it's accomplished, you feel satisfied. That's the magic of being a flow state.

Most of the time, instead of focusing on the task at hand, we get distracted by different things or find ourselves searching for something we can't quite put a finger on. Many people experience this, it's quite common. But how can you stay focused more on any given task? That's where the flow state greatly helps.

Work typically feels like a burdensome chore. But when you enter a flow state, even the most demanding job stops feeling like a burden.

For example, when I sit down to write, I am not always in the mood for writing. But then I'm also aware that if I just start and continue writing, I will eventually enter a flow state—and that's where the real magic happens. So, even for me, when I don't feel like writing for the day, I stick to my routine. Because once I sit down to write, I am able to do it regardless of my state of mind.

DO THE WORK THAT DOES NOT FEEL LIKE A CHORE.

Step-by-step guide to achieving flow state

There's no exact method or a guide that you can use to enter the flow state. It's may seem effortless, but it can also be quite challenging for some people.

For me, it happens quite naturally, especially while I am writing or meditating. I often find myself getting into the flow state during these activities. It ultimately depends on the person, what they truly believe in or enjoy doing.

Here's a step-by-step guide of how one can get into the flow state through an example of painting:

1. You gather all the necessary materials for painting.
2. You already have the image of what you want to create in your mind.
3. You start painting.
4. Here, your intentions matter a lot and gradually, you begin to focus.
5. After a while, you notice your mind is deeply involved and you're truly enjoying the process.

That's the simplest way of get into the flow state. Of course, there are other ways too, but it all depends on what works best for you.

Once you start doing it regularly, you will notice how your mindset shifts—from not liking it to actually liking it. This definitely needs practice, but once it becomes your routine, it gets easier to slip into that state daily.

That's the beauty of the flow state.

In a state of deep productivity

The number one rule to achieve a state of deep productivity has to be happiness. You have to enjoy the process. Without joy and fun, productivity will be meaningless.

Doesn't it feel amazing when you complete a task on time and also have fun while doing it? Your work shouldn't feel like a chore—it should feel almost effortless. That's exactly how you should go about accomplishing your daily tasks.

Truly productive people tend to track everything they do or plan to do because their primary goal is to save time. For them, time is one of the most valuable assets, and that is why many successful people delegate a good chunk of their routine work to the ones they trust so that they are free to do what truly matters to them.

YOUR INTENTIONS MATTER A LOT.

5

MASTER MENTAL TOUGHNESS

Building focus and productivity is easier said than done. Many people end up choosing wrong methods when it comes to improving their focus and attention. That's why it's important to have a clear strategy, especially when you have so several challenging tasks to do. Our brain is unique when it comes to understanding the difference between simple and tough tasks. There are several systems and techniques that help you do your tasks efficiently. But first, let's understand how our mind reacts to difficult tasks.

How our mind reacts to difficult tasks

Why do certain tasks feel so hard to carry out? If we carry out any task that requires a little more energy, our mind interprets it as hard, and we drop that task from our to-do list. We have gotten used to reacting this way, both psychologically and mentally.

Understanding why this happens can help you work on more difficult tasks, which eventually pushes you to grow and do better things in life. If you pay close attention, most of the time, our mind chooses easy tasks over tough ones. It always prefers comfort and avoids anything that feels too challenging.

We tend to get a little nervous and afraid before dealing with something difficult. That's when self-doubt sets in, leaving you feeling demotivated. This fear of failure and self-doubt hold you back from accomplishing the important, difficult tasks. And overcoming that fear and self-doubt is how you build mental toughness.

You vs. your mind

Our brain is incredibly complex. Now is the time you improve and understand how it works, especially while dealing with difficult tasks. It is high time you train your brain to choose hard tasks over simple ones.

Your brain will do what *you* want it to do. You must control your brain; don't let it control you. We are what we consistently do. If you let your brain make the decisions of choosing the tasks, your brain will always pick the easy one.

Train your brain to pick the tough tasks, as this will help you grow and improve.

When you tackle those challenges and overcome your fear, you will feel motivated and satisfied—that's what you need to grow and proceed in life.

You have several capabilities; all you simply need is consistency, and your mind will follow your lead.

YOUR MIND WILL DO WHAT YOU WANT IT TO DO.

Train your brain for growth

Our brain learns through repetition. If you do just one task repeatedly, your brain will learn this behaviour. It follows patterns through repeated actions. So, if you want to improve a habit, you simply need to do that activity regularly and consistently until your brain adapts to this pattern.

This can be achieved through small, persistent efforts. Remember, small habits can give you big results. That's the science behind compounding, and it can be applied to any area of your life.

You can build any habit by making these small efforts consistently. Over time, these small changes will bring out extraordinary results. If you want good results, then you should train your brain to be consistent.

Productivity is the result of cumulative small steps you take to achieve your goals. It's all about how you are using your mind to avoid challenges like fear, self-doubt, anxiety, and laziness in order to improve yourself.

When you push your limits, results will follow. You must prepare your mind before you start to build any habit, or take on any new task or a challenge. Push yourself slowly towards your goals. Give your brain some new challenges to learn and allow it to then improve and handle these challenges.

While facing these challenges and tough tasks, you will come across many failures. Your brain will see these failures as setbacks and try to demotivate you. But don't let your brain take over *you*. Consider them as feedback and learn from them. Every successful person in this world has failed several times, and emerged stronger by learning from those failures.

When you treat failures as feedback, you improve faster. In fact, failure is one of the most effective ways to grow, as long as you learn from it.

These are all small efforts and systems you can use to train your brain to pursue hard tasks. And when you do succeed, celebrate those wins and compare your personal growth from where you were to where you are now.

That's a great way to see how far you have come. Reflecting on your progress gives you confidence to take on future tasks and also complete them efficiently.

You must shift your perspective on difficult tasks. Do not see them as hurdles. Instead, see them as an opportunity to improve yourself. If you approach most of the hard tasks with this attitude, you're more likely to change your thinking.

Every challenge you face is an opportunity for you to learn something new and apply the skills to benefit your future.

PRODUCTIVITY LIES IN THE SMALL STEPS YOU TAKE TO ACHIEVE YOUR GOALS.

Working on a difficult task can be emotionally draining and your mind will tempt you to give up. Whenever you feel like giving up, try using positive self-talk. For example, you can use: "This is hard, but I can do this." This simple line can motivate you and give you that much-needed push to keep going.

All these strategies and tips will significantly increase your productivity, and also help you become more self-disciplined if you apply them consistently. Just remember to be patient with yourself when you apply these tips, and carry out each task with a positive mindset. The journey of personal growth takes time, but with a productive mindset and steady determination, you will reach your destination.

6

10 WAYS TO MASTER DAILY PRODUCTIVITY

Let's talk about daily productivity techniques that you can use in your everyday life. I will share some simple tips that can help you improve your work much faster. These are easy-to-implement techniques that are very effective. I personally use many of these based on the kind of work I'm doing.

1) S.M.A.R.T. goals

The S.M.A.R.T. goals is a framework quite popularly used as a productivity tool. People often use this method to define clear, actionable goals, and to ensure they are both achievable and effective.

- S = Specific
- M = Measurable
- A = Achievable
- R = Relevant
- T = Time-bound

Your goal should be *specific*. When your goal is clear in your mind, it becomes easier to achieve it. Instead of saying, "I want to build a reading habit," say "I will read a book for 30 minutes daily."

Defining your goals clearly and specifically can help you achieve more.

You should be able to track your goals. Make sure you *measure* your progress while you are working towards your goals. It's important to track them because this boosts your motivation to complete each goal.

Don't set unrealistic goals—like deciding to wake up at 5 a.m. when you usually get up at 10. Instead, set goals that challenge you but that you know are *achievable*. For instance, waking up at 9.30 a.m. instead of 10.

Your goals should be *relevant* to the larger objectives that you want to pursue in your life. Focus on what truly matters to you and set such goals that truly help you grow in your career.

Every goal you set should have a deadline. When you set a goal that's *time-bound,* it creates an urgency, so you act on it faster. It will also make you more consistent.

Use this S.M.A.R.T goals framework often, as it's quite effective and keeps you motivated. When you know how to use frameworks like this in your productivity toolbox, completing tasks and projects will become much easier.

2) The Eisenhower matrix

The Eisenhower matrix is another powerful productivity technique. This system helps you prioritise the tasks based on its urgency and importance.

You simply have to decide which task needs to be done based on the level of urgency and importance you have set for it. This system helps you focus better on what truly matters to you.

How Eisenhower Matrix works:

1) If it's urgent and important. (Do Now)
2) If not urgent but important. (Plan)
3) Urgent but not important. (Delegate)
4) Not urgent and not important. (Eliminate)

This approach gives you clarity enough to decide which task is meaningful, needs to be done promptly, and which task can be delegated and which one can be eliminated.

YOUR GOALS SHOULD BE RELEVANT TO THE LARGER OBJECTIVES YOU WANT TO PURSUE.

3. Find your peak productivity time

What time of the day are you most productive?

Everyone has a certain time in the day when their mind and body work the best. They perform much better during that hour with complete focus and energy as compared to the rest of the day.

If you schedule your productive task during these hours, where you are so focused and clear-headed, you are more likely to complete it efficiently. That's because your mind is sharp and focus is at its best.

For many people, their peak time is in the morning. For others, it might be in the evening or late night. It all depends on when you feel the most energised and focused.

Productivity is not only about finishing your tasks but also about how effectively and mindfully you do those tasks.

4. The 2-minute rule

The 2-minute rule is a widely used productivity technique that helps you overcome procrastination. This simple yet powerful technique says that if something takes less than two minutes to complete, you should do it immediately.

This rule is from a popular book by David Allen titled *Getting Things Done*. This technique is quite effective for quick and small tasks that require less energy. This method is also useful for forming any kind of habit.

Your focus increases when you follow this two-minute rule because it takes up very little time compared to other tasks. When you go through your to-do list, you can check all of the tasks that need less than two minutes to complete. You can pick the tasks according to the time and energy needed for them, and then complete them.

The two-minute rule helps you take immediate action, especially with small tasks. This method can help you build a lasting habit.

Completing a small task gives you a sense of accomplishment and boosts your confidence to take up bigger tasks. This will make you consistent in completing every task.

5. Time blocking

As mentioned in the previous chapter, time blocking is a productivity technique that involves setting aside a specific chunk of time for certain tasks and activities and managing your time throughout the day using tools such as your regular calendar or digital apps.

This is a great way to reduce distractions and increase your focus. When you dedicate a time slot for each of your tasks in your calendar, it becomes easier to carry them out. This, in turn, helps in reducing stress and staying focused throughout the day.

Plan your entire day, from the beginning to the end. Make sure you know which tasks and activities you want to complete and stick to this method without getting distracted to gain maximum output.

6. Task batching

Task batching is a unique and interesting technique where you group similar or related tasks and complete them in one-time block.

This method reduces the confusion and anxiety that arise when you are overwhelmed with numerous different activities. You get it all done by grouping similar types of tasks in one batch.

Try this for yourself: identify similar tasks, allocate them to a specific time block, and complete them in one go.

7. The Pomodoro technique

The Pomodoro technique is a time management method that involves taking short breaks after long, focused working sessions.

Developed by Francesco Cirillo in the late 1980s, this method is highly useful for boosting productivity, managing time, improving focus, and helping your brain reset and recover.

You start by selecting a task that you want to complete. Once you do that, then set a timer for 25 minutes—this is a standard Pomodoro work interval. You can set the timing as per your personal preference.

Now, work for straight 25 minutes, without getting distracted. Make sure you're in a quiet place while practising the Pomodoro method.

When the timer goes off, you must stop working and take a short five-minute break. This quick break helps you recharge your brain. You can relax, stretch your muscles, and take a quick walk, and so on. Just make sure you are refreshed and ready for your next session.

PRODUCTIVITY IS NOT ONLY ABOUT COMPLETING YOUR TASKS, IT IS ALSO ABOUT HOW EFFECTIVELY YOU CARRY OUT THOSE TASKS.

8. Kanban board

A Kanban board is a productivity tool used to manage your overall tasks and workflows. It is a visual project management system that clarifies each task by day and time, helping you understand when to carry them out during the day.

This system is widely used to organise your work better and visualize a clear path for all your tasks. It provides a clear overview of each task—you can track its status, and mark when to start or end the task.

You can create your personal Kanban board and add task cards, namely a *to-do list, review, status, progress,* and *completed.* This is a basic structure of a Kanban board, however, you can add cards as per your needs.

This visual board helps to streamline your entire workflow. You don't get to miss any of your work when you use this method. Your workload becomes lighter when you regularly create boards like this for your tasks. This board can be physical or digital, there are a lot of tools available to create the Kanban board. I urge you to read up about it and give it a try.

9. End-of-day review

An end-of-day review is a productivity technique in which you assess everything that you have worked on during the entire day. It involves looking at your every task—completed ones, unfinished ones, and whether to include them in your next to-do list or to delegate them. You simply reflect on your entire workday.

If you are not satisfied with the tasks you have completed on a particular day, you can plan for your next day and include your unfinished tasks in your next to-do list.

10. Productivity journaling

Productivity journaling is nothing but a system where you maintain a notebook or journal to stay accountable for your progress.

You can use it to write down your plans, track your goals, and effectively manage your time. This helps you to stay more focused and calm. When you write down your future goals, thoughts, and emotions, you feel good and motivated.

When used correctly, these journals help you

keep a track of your goals and daily progress. You can even track your habits consistently through journaling.

If you're not sure about what to write, I'd say keep it simple and stick to your plans and goals. If you write down unrelated and scattered thoughts and emotions, it won't particularly be helpful when it comes to achieving productivity in your tasks. Even better will be to maintain separate journals. One for your goals and another for jotting down your feelings and emotions.

Journaling technique is basically designed to improve yourself. If you include this productivity journaling in your routine, it will give you better control over your tasks and time, freeing your mind to focus on more exciting work.

7

QUALITY VS. QUANTITY

There is a common misconception that doing more equals achieving more. If you have completed many tasks in a day, you might feel that you've accomplished a lot. But being busy does not always mean that you do quality work. For instance, you could be working on a low-priority task that's less complex, instead of finishing a high-priority task with a fast-approaching deadline.

Many people keep themselves busy this way and believe that they had a productive day. But in reality, they have focussed on quantity over quality. You must ask yourself—how often have you felt truly satisfied with the work you have done? Probably not that often.

The illusion of busyness

You may often find yourself unable to make time for other important work or any other event because you are perpetually busy. But think about it: are you truly busy with your work, or is it something else that you are unable to see?

You may be working on three tasks at once but that doesn't make you productive. By doing multiple things at a time, you may not be able to complete even one of your tasks efficiently. That's because your focus gets scattered and the quality of work gets compromised.

However, working long hours just confuses your brain and it makes you believe that you are doing quality work. If you truly want to be productive and do quality work, just focus on a single task at a time.

Quality vs. quantity

If you assess your workflow, you may have realised that you haven't done any meaningful, quality work in the past several months. This realisation may lead to disappointment and may even trigger procrastination in some, eventually impacting their output. That's why quality of work matters over quantity. It also helps you enjoy the work you're doing.

Often, in a full-time workspace, you find yourself working on a task that's been assigned to you by your immediate superior whether you like it or not. Although you don't enjoy it, you have to finish the assigned task because it's your job. This obligation makes you lose interest in the task and you work on it for the sake of completing it.

Many people are stuck in this rut where they are not only dissatisfied with their job but also hate it. You are doing what's been told to you. There is no personal growth or development; no productive outcome. So, always prioritise quality over quantity.

Doing meaningful, quality work then doesn't feel like a tedious chore. That's because you choose to do that work, and enjoy it. This is the beauty of doing something intentionally. This consequently enhances the quality of the work you do, leaving you feeling truly satisfied and productive.

Let's look at this example. Two students are preparing for an exam. One of them spends six hours mugging up all the answers from the textbook with hardly any interest. The other spends only three hours willingly understanding the key concepts, practising problems, and reading all that's relevant for the exam.

Here, the first student did put in more time and effort, but did they actually learn anything meaningful in those six hours? Probably not, because they weren't interested in the subject and were studying only for the sake of the exam.

WHEN YOUR WORK FEELS MEANINGFUL, IT NO LONGER FEELS LIKE WORK.

While the student, who studied only for three hours, willingly took effort to understand the key concepts and read the relevant content for the exam in that short time.

Now, who do you think among the two is more likely to perform well in the exam? I'm sure you know the answer. However, to state the obvious, the second student would score better because they took interest in the subject (or, we can say that they liked the subject), while the first one clearly preferred mugging up because of lack of interest.

That said, do you know what the hard part in all this is? Figuring out what you like to do in order to do meaningful work. Many people struggle with this, but some have managed to find what they like.

You, too, must look within to identify what adds meaning to your life; things that give you positive vibes. This might be hard to notice at first, but if you want to do quality and meaningful work throughout your life, you simply have to keep looking for it.

WHEN YOU INTENTIONALLY DO SOMETHING MEANINGFUL, YOU'RE ALREADY IN LOVE WITH IT.

Tips to prioritise quality over quantity

1. Focus on what truly matters to you.
2. Delegate the tasks that are not so important.
3. Define your goals clearly and work towards achieving them.
4. Set your mindset to do meaningful work.
5. Focus deeper to get better output.
6. Follow your true intentions and emotions.
7. Focus on doing quality work—it brings joy.

Progress comes from slow productivity and taking small steps. Learn the science of how small habits lead to big results, and you will always be able to achieve your tasks. Cut out non-essential tasks from your list to make time for important ones.

I always try to focus on tasks that give me joy as well as meaningful experience. I see to it that those tasks are also aligned with my long-term goals. Similarly, if you have set a long-term goal, you can focus on the tasks that lead you to achieve those long-term goals. This not only adds value to your daily life but also makes you prioritise quality over quantity.

8

FOCUS THROUGH MEDITATION

Our lifestyle today has become quite sedentary and unhealthy in many ways. Almost everyone who is reading this book will have once found themselves in an endless rabbit hole of doomscrolling, binge watching, and binge eating. This not only disrupts our physical health but also our mental peace, making it harder for us to stay productive and focus on the things we need to do.

In order to get out of this vortex of bad habits, we should take it upon ourselves to consciously stay motivated. It's not easy, but surely not impossible.

To be honest with you, there are days when I feel demotivated and don't do any of my tasks. That's when I realise that I need some time to cool off. I head out of home or the environment

I am in and take a break. As soon as I understand that my body and brain need a break, I pause and recharge. As simple as that.

Almost all of us dream of having a stress-free job or working without pressure. Yet, many people can't do this because of constant mental stress and self-doubt.

You can be more productive and focused when your mind and body are aligned with your thoughts and intentions, that's why you need some meaningful breaks sometimes. Meditation is one such meaningful break you should take.

Meditation helps increase your focus

Ever wondered why meditation helps so many people in different areas of their lives? I have seen many successful people include mindfulness in their daily routine. It is because meditation is one of the most natural ways to improve our life. It strengthens our mind-body connection.

There have been scientific studies backing how meditation can improve our focus and attention. Practising it regularly transforms our overall well-being. Once you grasp the technique, you will notice that it reduces your stress and you will start tackling your tasks with sharper focus and renewed energy.

LIFE BECOMES EASIER WHEN WE KEEP THINGS SIMPLE AND DON'T OVERCOMPLICATE THEM.

How meditation changed my life

Meditation was something I had never really explored earlier. In fact, I used to make fun of the people who meditated daily. However, it was only a few years ago that I started practising regularly. I never knew this simple practice could change my life forever. And now that I am aware of its wonderful benefits, I regret not starting it sooner.

I was first introduced to meditation by my uncle. He practised it daily and often spoke passionately about its benefits. At the time, I didn't take it seriously. I would listen, nod, and quickly forget about it. Still, he continued to encourage me, reminding me how powerful meditation could be for both the mind and body. One day, out of curiosity, I decided to give it a try. After just one session, I felt a surprising sense of calm and clarity that I hadn't experienced before.

From that moment on, meditation became a regular part of my life.

I have been practising mindfulness meditation for the last three years. It has had a positive impact on my mind, body, and thought process. My concentration, focus, and discipline have increased a lot. I now take better decisions with a focused mind.

What I like about meditation is that it benefits tremendously when you practise it with strong intentions towards your goals.

You get positive thoughts no matter the challenging situation you are in or even when someone isn't treating you well. Your mind just focuses on positive things and makes you think about how you can face adverse situations with a calm mind.

Whether or not you currently meditate, my advice would be to just give it a try.

Mindfulness meditation is quite useful when you are stressed or anxious about something. You carry stress, anxiety, and self-doubt with you unnecessarily for a long time. Your needlessly overthink on negative thoughts and feelings. Mindfulness meditation is one of the best ways to get out of this whirlpool of misery.

If you haven't done meditation in your life and want to start, you can practise every day by doing it regularly for a few minutes. In the beginning, you will easily get distracted and would not be able to sit still because your body and mind have not developed this habit yet. But once you do it regularly and your body adapts to meditation, you will be able to meditate with ease.

When it comes to productivity—or anything in life—my motto is: "Once you set your mind to it, you can do anything."

ONCE YOU SET YOUR MIND TO IT, YOU CAN DO ANYTHING.

Become the best version of yourself

Meditation isn't about becoming a different person—it's about becoming the best version of yourself.

You can transform yourself completely, and meditation helps you do that by guiding you to your true self. It's not about losing your identity, but it's a way of reconnecting and expressing yourself.

It's the best connection between mind, body, and breath. When these three are well aligned, your brain works at its best.

Think about it: whenever you decide to go into a full productive mode, you suddenly notice a lot of things that are competing for your attention. From a small beep of your phone notifications to blaring background noises, all these external things easily manage to distract you from even beginning your task in the first place, let alone completing it.

You must build a mental fortress around you whenever you sit down to work so that no one can have the power to take that away from you. Meditation is that powerful tool that helps you build such a mental fortress, allowing you to work without any distractions.

You must believe in this force of power that will always be with you. Distractions caused by external forces are fleeting, they don't impact you or care about your intentions. But once you realise and believe in this power of meditation and start practising regularly, it will help you develop a strong internal force to overcome any mental and emotional hurdles.

You can apply numerous tips and tricks to help yourself, but you only live a true, meaningful life when you identify this internal force and live consciously and mindfully.

9

POWER OF THE RIGHT MINDSET

A right mindset is what everyone needs to grow in life. You can be good at something, but you need the right mindset to stay consistent. If you lack clarity, hold on to rigid thoughts, overthink, or engage in negative self-talk, you will struggle to realise your true potential.

You need to develop a mindset that helps you overcome these challenges.

Start with the right mindset

Start by thinking that you're going to do a task no matter the challenges and distractions you face; this way, you set yourself on the right track.

A right mindset helps you to flourish in your life. It empowers you with a powerful vision that will guide you throughout your life.

The more you focus on building a right mindset, the more you will grow. Maintaining a disciplined routine helps a lot when we have goals to accomplish.

Follow these steps to build the right mindset:

1. Have a goal in mind.
2. Focus on what will help you achieve it.
3. Don't stop working towards your goal.
4. Be consistent, no matter how hard it is.
5. Believe in steady progress.

You must have probably heard this phrase—life is a race—several times. But it's true; everyone is competing with one another to achieve something in life. Some people chase big goals, some aim for small goals, but everyone aspires to achieve something or the other.

If you want to stay focused in this distracted world, you must make your mindset your strength. Make sure you deeply care about your goal and work hard for it.

YOU DON'T FEEL MOTIVATED ENOUGH, IF YOU'RE NOT CLEAR ABOUT YOUR GOALS.

I practise what I share with you. I have been doing it regularly and can see huge improvements in myself and have good clarity towards my goals.

If you haven't set any goals in life, you won't have a direction in life. It's never too late to set any goals in life. Most of the successful people who have achieved something great in their lives set goals and achieve them with a right mindset.

Everything needs practice; and to achieve this right mindset, all you have to do is practice.

10

THE ART OF DOING NOTHING

Did you know that doing nothing can make you more productive?

In this chapter, I'm going to suggest something quite the opposite of what I normally recommend. You may be wondering what's gotten into me. But hear me out—doing nothing is emerging as one of the newest approaches of achieving productivity.

This doesn't mean that you shouldn't try anything at all; it means everything life will happen naturally and effortlessly once you stop being hard on yourself.

The art of not trying

This is a new technique you can explore, but it has nothing to do with your actual work and productive lifestyle.

It's a new approach to life. How you live, act, and do your work.

This approach is not about taking any action, but it's about taking the right type of action. You will do the right thing that will not take any effort, but will, in fact, be effective.

This is the psychology between the action and the break. How you treat your body naturally and take rest matters a lot.

It is not about "not trying" but knowing when to stop. It should come to you naturally, just like being in the flow state. You can relate to this if you have experienced the flow state.

You can say, I like doing nothing. But there's a lot happening in that nothingness. It's a natural way of doing things that are connected to your intentions.

It's just the same thing as "doing less to achieve more." Living effortlessly and achieving more.

It is Chinese philosopher Lao Tzu's philosophy I read in his book *Tao Te Ching*. It's a beautiful philosophy of not fighting with nature's flow of events that happen in our lives, instead, aligning with its flow.

Trust the process and don't be in a rush to achieve everything at once. It's a slow process, but you'll get what you are aiming for.

For example, when you sit quietly, simply observe your thoughts or enjoy the calm around you. It may seem like you're doing nothing, but internally, your mind is resting, recharging, and often connecting ideas without you even realising it. Some of the best ideas—whether for work, life, or creativity—often come when you're not actively chasing them, but when you're relaxed and letting them flow naturally. It's in this stillness that real movement happens.

Think about a busy professional who steps away from their desk to take a slow walk outside, without their phone or any agenda. While they seem to be "doing nothing," their mind is processing tasks, organising priorities, and finding solutions in the background. When they return to work, they're sharper, more focused, and able to solve problems faster than if they had kept forcing themselves to sit and think.

The person who follows simplicity is the one who lives in harmony with everyone. Focus on being simple, not complex.

THE PERSON WHO FOLLOWS SIMPLICITY IS THE ONE WHO LIVES IN HARMONY WITH EVERYONE.

We are influenced by so many people around the world. We mould our lifestyle according to the newest viral trends.

In this new approach, you're not forcing yourself to do anything. This is not the kind of method you are trying to get things done faster.

It's a game of letting things be done effortlessly; you can try to do it but don't force yourself to do the things.

If something is not achievable or you're trying too hard but it's not happening, you can drop it and do it some other time. But don't push yourself too hard to complete the task—give it time and space.

If you want to live happily, just try this approach one day and decide whether you like it or not. Sit in silence and don't force yourself to do any task. If something comes your way, do it, otherwise, don't try to do anything by yourself.

You will learn a lot about yourself by using this method.

People who live like this believe in minimalism and simplicity. This sounds like fun to do, but it's quite the opposite.

It can be challenging to live this way enjoying

life while letting go of most things but you'll find yourself even happier because of it.

I sometimes try to live like this; it's a beautiful experience, living with the flow of nature.

It's a belief that you can do anything if you align with the true nature of the flow state. You can be one with your natural state.

To give you an example, here's how I spend my day: I start my day by slowing down—no rushing, no cramming tasks into every minute. For me, I choose only a few things that truly matter to me that day, and let the rest fall away without guilt. As I move through the day, I act with intention, whether I am working, resting, or simply sitting in silence. I focus fully on each moment without worrying about the next. I spend time in nature if I want, breathe deeply, and appreciate small, ordinary things like a good conversation, a meal, a walk, and so on.

Resist the urge to chase more, instead trust that whatever you need will come naturally. By the end of the day, you'll find that in doing less, you actually lived more and touched a kind of peace and happiness that effort alone can't create.

For workaholics who are obsessed about their

daily tasks and have this compulsive need to check off every task on their to-do list, this approach may not suit them well.

However, people who are not in a hurry to finish their to-do list, have more liberty of time, and do not rely on others for their job, will find this technique quite useful.

Do try this technique for a day and see it for yourself.

YOU CAN DO ANYTHING IF YOUR ACTIONS ALIGN WITH THE TRUE NATURE OF THE FLOW STATE.

11

17 HABITS OF HIGHLY PRODUCTIVE PEOPLE

1. Going to bed early

Most highly productive people hit the sack early in order to wake up early the next morning. It's a routine that many of them follow with complete discipline. They give their bodies the rest they deserve after a long, tiring day and prepare themselves for the next day.

2. Having clarity of purpose

If you notice, most successful people have clearly defined goals. They know their purpose. If you lack clarity, you'll always struggle to achieve your goals. Make sure you have a list of the things that you want to achieve for the day or month.

3. Building consistency

Everything needs practice. You can't build any habit just by doing it once. You must do it consistently for a couple of months at least to build a habit or improve a skill.

Highly productive people follow this consistency formula and use it to build new habits.

4. Choosing progress over perfection

Aim for continuous progress instead of chasing perfection. There's no such thing as perfection, it will only add more stress if you are unable to complete your tasks perfectly.

If you think you are perfect, you'll stop growing in life. Accept your flaws. Just focus on slow, steady growth.

5. Making a clear to-do list

Having a focused to-do list helps you stay accountable for everything you do. It allows you to track all your tasks.

It's important to arrange your tasks according to their priority, and have a clear to-do list.

6. Maintaining a good sleep routine

A good night's sleep helps your body relax on a deeper level. It also enhances your brain; you think more logically, and improves your focus on the various tasks that are important to you.

An 8-9 hour sleep routine takes you to a peaceful state of mind, where you think more clearly and calmly.

7. Having a strong mindset

A right mindset is what you need the most. When you are determined that you're going to achieve a goal, your mind already believes it.

If you have a strong mindset, your brain will never disappoint you in making any decision or completing any task.

8. Limiting distractions

If you want to be productive, you must organise your environment according to it. Your place needs to be free of distractions.

Pick a quiet place for your productive work. Keep your phone in another room, and make sure no one comes and distracts you when you're working on your tasks.

9. Knowing their capabilities

You need to know what you're capable of and believe in yourself that you can do anything. When you push yourself to the limits, that's when you know your capabilities.

You're more than enough.

10. Staying clean and organised

Most productive people make sure they are organised and presentable. Being clean and having a decluttered environment helps your mind to calm down and gain good clarity.

This habit of staying organised and decluttering ensures that you're on the right path towards becoming one of the highly productive people.

11. Focusing on a growth mindset

I strongly believe in a growth mindset. If you have this mindset, no one can stop you from achieving anything.

People who have achieved greatness in life have one thing in common—they all believe in a growth mindset in everything. It's the key to becoming truly successful in life.

12. Surrounding themselves with positive people

Your life is heavily influenced by the company you keep and things you surround yourself with.

Spend your time with positive people so that you develop a positive approach towards life and have good energy around you.

13. Reading self-help books

If you are reading this book, it may mean that you like reading self-help books. But if you don't read regularly, you will soon break this habit. You need to be consistent with reading.

Build a habit of reading at least two pages a day if you're just starting. Self-help books can enlighten you in your overall personal development.

14. Being a good listener

A highly productive person is always a good listener. They are interested in broadening their perspective and have keen interest in knowing what the other person has to say.

Many people often make the mistake of responding too quickly before attentively listening to the next person. This is a bad communication technique, as the other person doesn't feel heard and can even put them off.

You should listen first and then reply. Good communication is not about replying; it's about listening actively first.

15. Practising daily gratitude

Be thankful for what you have. Gratitude is one of the best things that you can practise if you want to live a peaceful, happy, and meaningful life. It trains your attention and focus on the good things that you already have, rather than fretting about what you don't. This helps in developing the right mindset for achieving your goals.

16. Meditating daily

As discussed in the earlier chapter, meditation helps in your overall development. If you include it in your daily routine, it can enhance your productivity.

Several successful people swear by setting some time aside a few minutes daily for meditation—it keeps their mind clear, focused, and calm.

17. Not being afraid of taking risks

If you don't take risks, you won't achieve anything meaningful in life. This is not to say that you have to take risky decisions all the time.

It simply means you may have to first assess your situation and then take some calculated risks in life while making certain decisions. Don't shy away from them. Have the courage to face them—otherwise, life is not worth living.

**A RIGHT MINDSET
IS WHAT YOU NEED
THE MOST.**

12

27 LIFE LESSONS FROM 27 YEARS OF MY LIFE

1. Don't overthink, act now!

Don't waste too much time on thinking about consequences or worrying about what has not happened yet. If you want to start something, don't overanalyse, do it as soon as you feel right.

When you are young, you don't think about failure that often. You just dive into the task without that fear of failure. So, do that even today. If you fail, you'll learn and come up even stronger.

2. Collect meaningful memories

Good memories are what you should always aim to collect. Spend quality time with your close friends and family members and create good memories.

Time is flying by quickly; once gone, it won't return. So, we should use this time to spend with our loved ones and make good memories.

3. Create personal productivity methods

There are many popular productivity techniques out there like the Pomodoro Technique, Time Blocking, and the Eisenhower Matrix. Not every method will fit your unique style, energy levels, or lifestyle. That's why it's important to experiment and create a personal productivity system that works specifically for you.

You might even find that working in 50-minute deep-focus blocks suits you better than the classic 25-minute Pomodoro sessions. Or that planning just three important tasks each day feels more natural than managing a long to-do list.

4. Build good habits

One of the best self-help improvements is building good habits. They help shape your daily routine, bring discipline to your life, and over time, change your mindset. This, in turn, boosts your overall personal growth and productivity.

5. Start journaling

I have always been a proponent of journaling. Writing down your thoughts help you gain clarity and lets you introspect about your daily actions.

Journaling makes you self-aware. It helps you ease your stress and anxiety once you write down all the thoughts and emotions that burden you. It helps you look into your true self. If you haven't put down your thoughts on paper, do try for a few days and see the benefits for yourself.

6. Talk less, work more

Don't just talk endlessly about your work or life with everyone, focus more on upskilling and building yourself. You should not brag about your goals or challenges to prove a point to someone. If you really want to do something in life, go and achieve that damn thing.

Don't waste energy on explaining what you're up to. Oversharing with people actually ruins our efforts as we come under the pressure of expectations. So, talk less and let your work talk for you.

7. Move out of your comfort zone

You're never going to be successful if you can't leave your comfort zone. We are so used to living in comfort that we tend to be lazy and don't venture out.

We learn a lot about ourselves as well as our capacity to succeed if we just leave our comfort zone.

IF YOU WANT TO START SOMETHING, DON'T OVERANALYSE, DO IT AS SOON AS YOU FEEL RIGHT.

8. Your actions today impact your future

If you want a better future, don't just sit back and watch others become successful and live their best lives. Wake up and smell the coffee. Do what you're best at; start creating your best life.

9. Focus on creating value first; profit will follow

The most sustainable way to succeed in business, career, or life is to create real value first. Instead of chasing money directly, identify a genuine problem people face and offer a meaningful solution. When you focus on helping others, profit becomes a natural outcome.

People are willing to pay when they see their problems being solved or their lives improving.

10. Focus on your interest

You should always do what you are interested in. People get disheartened and lose their motivation to work when they do something they don't even like doing.

Find out what you are interested in, and you will always be happier doing your work.

11. True relationships matter in life

There is nothing more important than a true relationship. A meaningful relationship is like a self-healing system, which can help you recover you from anything.

Build relationships like the one you want to have. It's truly amazing if you have a relationship like this in your life. Value it.

12. Read a book a month

Books are still so underrated when it comes to improving oneself. One book has tremendous power to transform your life for the better. If you just pick the right book at the right time, it can be a life-changing experience for you.

Start with reading self-help books. They are great for beginners. You learn so many things in just a short amount of time; they truly enlighten you. Try reading at least one book a month and see it for yourself.

13. Spend time with yourself

You can learn more about your thoughts and emotions if you just spend a little time with yourself. Many people don't know what they like or dislike. It's because they simply don't spend enough time with their thoughts.

If you don't know yourself well enough, you'll simply get confused most of the time while taking crucial decisions in your life.

HAVE GOOD INTENTIONS BEHIND EVERYTHING YOU DO. PEOPLE WILL APPRECIATE IT, AND SUCCESS WILL FOLLOW.

14. Focus on one goal at a time

Focus on doing one thing at a time. People try to do many things, that's why they get distracted and lag behind or don't complete their work.

Just focus on the most important task for the day and complete it.

15. Every minute is worth living

Life is an experience, a journey that needs to be explored every minute with love, joy, and curiosity.

Life isn't just about work, love, marriage, or growing old—it's much more than that. You must embrace each moment and go with the flow.

16. Set strong intentions

When you work on a task or do something with strong intentions and emotions, you are more likely to get that thing done. Intentions are so powerful; they guide your actions to fruition. So, make sure you set your intentions well before starting the job.

17. Invest in yourself

Spend on yourself in order to improve in areas that you feel can do better in. For instance, spending on books, fitness, and courses that help you upskill and grow.

Taking care of your physical and mental health is quite crucial, and investing in yourself will help with your overall development.

18. It's okay if you haven't figured out everything yet

You don't need to compulsively figure everything out in your life. The problem is you think everyone is so ahead of you and they've their life sorted, which is not always true.

We all are learning, trying, and failing. Life is never simple; everything takes time and effort on your part. When the time is perfect, you'll figure it out yourself.

19. Find happiness in simple things

How often do you find yourself being happy doing complex things? Happiness is a state of mind; you can be happy just right now, wherever you are. It doesn't rely on big success or events.

You can find joy even in the simplest and smallest of things. You can be happy right now reading this book; it's just that simple.

20. Learn to detach from things

Have you ever wondered why you get so upset when someone hurts you?

You have attached yourself so deeply to everything that your emotions are no longer under your control.

The emotions get the better of you and cloud your decisions.

You must learn of ways to detach yourself. It's a gradual process, but you can start practising as early as possible.

21. Listen more, speak less

Whether in relationships or business, active listening earns trust and respect. People remember those who truly hear them, not those who dominate conversations. Active listening opens doors, reveals opportunities, and builds deeper connections.

YOU CAN EARN

MONEY, BUT NOT TIME.

SO, USE IT WISELY.

22. Travel more

If you have the means and resources, travel often. Visiting new places, meeting different people, and familiarising yourself with new cultures can shape your experiences and perspective on life and society.

Your mindset broadens, and you see positive changes in your thinking and behaviours. It also serves as a good and refreshing escape from your mundane life and enriches your soul. Everyone should at least take one long trip in a year if possible.

23. Increase your digital presence

As you may be well aware, our present and future belong to technology and media. If you don't learn and adapt, you'll be left behind. Today, everyone is trying to make their presence felt in the digital space.

You should, too, start putting yourself out there. You can start with writing a blog, publishing a book, create content online, or anything you're good at. Try to build an audience and be consistent with it. You'll be glad one day that you started it.

24. Stillness is the key

Stillness is a stoic practice followed by many stoic philosophers in the past for better clarity and peace.

Don't try to complete multiple tasks at once. You won't be able to do all the year's work in one day. Just sit back and relax. Take some time out, pause, and be still.

Life becomes meaningful when you just sit and reflect on the things you love. When you practise stillness, your body and soul are also in a still mode and help you to be in a happier state.

25. Fake it till you make it

Sometimes, you need to pretend to be good at something until you learn it completely.

Use this trick till you make sure you become quite good at it. This is similar to manifesting what we truly want in life. I have used this method many times in my life effectively. You should give it a go as well.

26. Learn how to express yourself

Many young people nowadays struggle with expressing their feelings and emotions. That hinders their growth and learning curve.

You need to learn how to communicate effectively so that you can build good relationship with others. Learn and practise how to express yourself articulately.

27. Value time

Once gone, you will never be able to replace or turn back time. If you understand the importance of time early in life, you'll make better choices.

You can earn money but not time. So, use it wisely.

ABOUT THE AUTHOR

Ravi Saroj is the creator behind Mindset Reading, a well-known self-improvement channel on social media, with a community of over 8,00,000 readers.

A passionate reader, writer, and content creator, Ravi holds a bachelor's degree in computer engineering. Through Mindset Reading, he shares insights on personal growth, productivity, and the power of mindset.

To know more about Ravi and Mindset Reading:

Instagram: @mindsetreading

X: @mindsetreading

JAICO PUBLISHING HOUSE

Elevate Your Life. Transform Your World.

ESTABLISHED IN 1946, Jaico Publishing House is home to world-transforming authors such as Robin Sharma, Sadhguru, Osho, the Dalai Lama, Deepak Chopra, Eknath Easwaran, Paramhansa Yogananda, Devdutt Pattanaik, Radhakrishnan Pillai, Morgan Housel, Napoleon Hill, John Maxwell, Brian Tracy, and Stephen Hawking.

Our late founder Mr. Jaman Shah first established Jaico as a book distribution company. Sensing that independence was around the corner, he aptly named his company Jaico ('Jai' means victory in Hindi). In order to service the significant demand for affordable books in a developing nation, Mr. Shah initiated Jaico's own publications. Jaico was India's first publisher of paperback books in the English language.

While self-help; religion and philosophy; mind, body and spirit; and business titles form the cornerstone of our non-fiction list, we publish an exciting range of current affairs, history, biography, art and architecture, travel, and popular science books as well. Our renewed focus on popular fiction is evident in our new titles by a host of fresh young talent from India and abroad.

Jaico's translations division publishes select bestselling titles in over 10 regional languages including Gujarati, Hindi, Kannada, Malayalam, Marathi, Tamil, and Telugu. These include titles from renowned national and international authors like Sudha Murthy, Gaur Gopal Das, Swami Mukundananda, Jay Shetty, Simon Sinek, Ankur Warikoo and Jeff Keller.

Visit our Website

Boasting one of India's largest book distribution networks, Jaico has its headquarters in Mumbai, with branches in Ahmedabad, Bangalore, Chennai, Delhi, Hyderabad, and Kolkata. This network ensures that our books reach all parts of the country, both urban and rural.